PHP Programming For Beginners

The Simple Guide to Learning PHP Fast!

Table Of Contents

Introduction

I want to thank you and congratulate you for downloading the book PHP Programming for Beginners.

This book contains proven steps and strategies on how to become a truly competent user of PHP programming. You will learn how to get started with it, how it works, and when to use it.

If you do not develop your PHP skills, it may slow your blogging and website production. It is very popular and powerful, and it has the ability to make your website one of the most well-known and visited sites.

It's time for you to become an amazing web-developer and PHP expert. This book is geared towards beginners, and it will offer some basic tutorials on how you can get started. You will learn the basics about PHP programming, what it is used for, who will benefit from it and how you can begin using it as well. PHP programming has the power to be more efficient with your web designing, and it will give you the ability to interact with visitors on your site. It is time to take your programming to new heights, and impress people who are visiting your site. You will learn one of the most efficient ways to implement coding, thus making your work much easier.

Chapter 1:
Back to Basics

Looking to create an impressive new website? You should consider trying PHP coding, especially if you're new to web development. It serves a lot of functions, and it can complete a lot for you and your website. It is currently the only program that utilises open server side programs. It's also fun and simple to use too. In addition, it is suitable for up-to-date XML application, and it will allow you to create your own modules. Furthermore, you can use it with a server such as Apache. First of all, you can use it for:

1. Server-side scripting: This is the most basic and main field for PHP. However, in order for this to work you will need the PHP parser (a CGI or server module) and a web server and a web browser that has a connected PHP installation. You can get access to a PHP program output with a web browser, and you can view the PHP page through the server. All of these programs will work on your home computer, especially if you're wanting to learn PHP programming on your own.

2. Command line scripting: You can make a PHP script run without using a server or browser. This makes it very user friendly, and you only need a PHP parser if you want to use it without a server or browser. It is good to use this type of scripting if you execute your scripts using cron (which is on nix or Linux) or Task Scheduler (which is on Windows). Additionally, it can also be used for simple text processing tasks.

3. Writing desktop applications: PHP may not the best choice or the best language if you're creating a desktop

application with a graphical user interface. However, if you are familiar with PHP applications, and you want to use some advanced features with it inside your client-side applications, then you can use PHP-GTK to write the programs. Moreover, you will be able to write cross-platform applications this way too.

So what exactly is PHP? For starters, it is a server-side language that is used specifically for web development, and it can be used as a general purpose programming language. It can also be used in combination with HTML or other template engines. It is known as "Hypertext Pre-Processor" and you can use it to create usernames and even login pages. It is suitable for anyone who blogs and would like to create forums, galleries and even surveys.

Getting Started

One thing you have to remember with PHP is that it will let you insert PHP codes in HTML coded sites, and you can complete the inserted PHP coding when someone requests your page. PHP coding is closed off within unique start and finish tags, such as:

```
<?php
... Your PHP code...
?>
```

This is another example that will show you how you can combine both of these types of coding

```
<html>

<head></head>

<body>

Person: So what is your name, anyway?
<br />

<? php
// print output
echo 'Jack: I am Jack, but my friends have nicknamed me The Joker.';
?>

</body>

</html>
```

Once you're done that, you can save that somewhere in your document that has a .php connection. You can browse for it, and you should see this:

Person: So what is your name, anyway?

Jack: I am Jack, but my friends have nicknamed me The Joker.

When you request the script, Apache will receive the request and send it to the PHP. PHP interprets the script, and executes the coding in between the marks and it replaces it with your output from the coding. This information is sent back to your server and sent to your client. As long as the output has valid HTML, then it should be displayed by the user.

If you take a closer look, you will notice that every PHP has a semicolon at the end. It is important to leave it, and many people make the mistake of deleting it. However, you should remember that you don't need the semicolon to delete the line at the end of the PHP script. You can even add commentaries to the PHP code, and PHP understands one line and multi-line comments such as:

```php
<?php
// a one line one comment
/* this line has more
Than one
sentence*/
?>
```

If there are blank lines, the PHP labels will be overlooked by your parser, as well as anything outside the tags. It will only read the code that is inside the tags. Another important thing to remember is that PHP utilises variables. You can think of a variable as a type of programming builder that can store data with numbers, and without numbers. You can change the subject of the variable when you're executing the program. Furthermore, you can compare the variables too. Therefore, you can write the code that will perform the actions based on the comparison.

PHP is also compatible with other variable types, such as floating point numbers, integers, as well as arrays and strings. It is important that you specify which variable type you are using before you implement it. One example is if you are using an integer, you need to specify it as a type of integer. In PHP programming, a dollar symbol goes before the name of a variable, and it has to start with a letter or an underscore. It can be followed by other numbers, letters, and underscores if you wish. One example is $saturday, which is a correct PHP variable name, however something like $456 or $24hrs is not valid. In addition, variable names can vary depending on whether it is upper case or lower case, so a variable like $you is different from $You or $YOU. One example of PHP's variables is:

```php
<html>

<head></head>

<body>
Person: So what is your name, anyway?

<br />
<? php

// define variables

$Person = 'Jack';
$type = 'Anomaly';

$Number = 1;
// print output

echo "Jack: I am <b>$name</b>, the <b>$type</b>. You can refer to me by my number, <b>$Number</b>.";
```

```
?>
```

```
</body>
```

```
</html>
```

In this example, the variables $person, $type and $Number are characterised with both strings and number values, and after that they are replaced in the function that is called echo. The echo function and the print function serve to print the information to the original output device. You can also include the HTML tags within the call to echo tags, as well as anything else in your browser.

Assigning a value

If you want to assign something to a value, you have to use the operator: the=symbol. It will assign a value (which is to the right of your equation) to a variable (which is to the left of your equation). The subject that you're assigning does not always have to be fixed, and it can be another expression, variable or an expression that involves other variables:

```
<?php
$age = $dob + 15;
?>
```

You can complete multiple functions at a time. The example below gives three variables one value at the same time.

```
<?php
```

You should note that every type of language will have various types of variables. The language will support a vast array of data, which includes string and Boolean types, numbers, characters as well as other objects. This is the list of the basic ones:

Boolean- This is the most basic variable type, and it specifies whether a value is wrong or right.

Integer: As the name suggests, it is a simple number like 85, or 1000

Floating point: A number that is floating point is usually a fraction such as 13.5 or 3.14. They may be indicated with a decimal or a scientific notation.

String: This is an arrangement of characters, such as "goodbye" or "nothing". String values can be closed with either types of quotes, such as ("") or ('). The quotation marks can be in the string alone, or it can escape by a backslash (\). If you're using string values in quotes that are doubled, they will be automatically checked for unique characters and names. Once they are located, they can be exchanged with the right value like in this example:

```
<?php
$identity = 'John Doe';

$vehicle = 'Mercedes';
// this would contain the string "John Doe drives a Mercedes"

$sentence = "$identity drives a $vehicle";

echo $sentence;
?>
```

What Are Operators?

You can think of operators as the adhesive that you can build something with. PHP has operators that are used for string, arithmetic, and comparison and logical operations. Are you wanting to get more comfortable with using operators? For starters, you can use them to achieve arithmetic operations on your variables.

It may seem complex, but it is actually easy to understand. Let us start from the beginning, which is where the variables for unit cost as well as the quantity are. The next thing you have to do is the calculations using PHP's various mathematical operations, and the results are stored in various data. The remainder of your script is connected to what your results show in an organized table. Alternatively, you can achieve an operation that is arithmetic at the same time as the assignment, and you can use the operators together. One example of this is:

```php
<?php
// this...

$a = 5;

$a = $a + 10;
// ... is the same as this

$a = 5;

$a += 10;
?>
```

Chapter 2:
Stringing Along

PHP will also allow you to increase strings along with your operator with something that is called a string concatenation, which has a period. Forms are a quick and simple way for you to interact on your website. For example, if you are selling a product, you will be able to use a form to ask consumers to rate your product, and you can ask casual visitors to leave feedback on your website. PHP can make this easy for you, and it does this by giving out the data you get from the form.

The "action tribute" of the form tag will specify the name of the server-side script, and it will process the information that is entered into the form. The method attribute will specify how to pass the information. The other half (which is the message.php. script) will read the data that you send and it will do something about it.

You can enter some information into the form.htm, and then you can send it. Your message that is the form processor will interpret it, and then display it for you. For example, if you want it to say "hi", then it will read back to you: ("You said: Hi"). Therefore, whenever you send a form to a script, all the pairs that are part of the form will be ready to use right away inside the script in a specific container variable, such as $_POST. After that, you can get the number of the variable by utilising the name that is in the $_POST container. PHP accepts the GET method from the form submission, and all you have to do is alter the "method" attribute to "get" and then you can generate values from $_GET instead of $_POST. These variables are a unique type of PHP script which is referred to as an array.

Now that we have gone over the easy commands, it is time to build what is called a "conditional statement". This is a statement that will allow your script to perform a number of likely actions that are built on your results of the comparison. However, you have to be able to compare both variables in order to determine if they are similar or not. The language that you're using includes operators that that are designed to compare both of your values.

The result of the test will always be Boolean, and it will either be true or false. False will not print anything. Comparison operators will be an integral part of the PHP programming, and you can utilise it with a statement that is conditional to transmit your script using any of the several action paths. Moreover, the 4.0 version of PHP has a new operator to do comparisons, and it will let you test the type and equality. The operator is exemplified in this equation:

```
<? php
It will define two variables
$str = '15';

$int = 15;
```

It will come back as true, because they have the same number

The uses of PHP don't just stop there, but you can use it for logical operators, and they are used to bring together expressions that are conditional. The four operators are: logical XOR, logical OR, logical AND as well as logical NOT, which is exemplified below:

```
<?php
/* define some variables */
$name = 1;
```

```php
$day = 1;

$type = 4;
/* logical AND will come back as correct if the statements are true

// comes back as correct

$result = (($name == 1) && ($day! = 0));

print "result is $result<br />";
/* it can logical or correct if any of your conditions are correct
// will come back as correct
$result = (($day== 1) || ($type <= 2));

print "result is $result<br />";
/* It will come back as false or incorrect */

// will come back as false

$result = !($day == 1);

it will print you the result, and it will have a dollar sign in front of it.
/* the logical XOR will come back as true if any of your conditions
are correct, or it will come back as false if any of your conditions are
correct */

// will return false
$result = (($day == 1) xor ($name == 1));

it will print you the result, and it will have a dollar sign in front of it.
?>
```

The logical operators are important in creating conditional statements, and they are utilised to bring together conditions that are related easily.

Chapter 3:
More Fun With Statements

A statement that is conditional will let you test whether or not a certain situation is factual or untrue, and it will take various actions that are based on the result. The simplest way you can use the conditional statement is in the if statement mode, which looks like:

```
if (condition) {

    Complete this!

}
```

The if ( ) is conditional, and it will determine if the operation is factual or untrue. If the comment is factual, all of your PHP codes within the braces are executed, and if it doesn't the code inside the braces are missed and the outlines succeeding the if ( ) function are implemented. Below you will see an example of how this statement works when you combine it to the form. For example if you ask someone how old he or she is.

```
<html>

<head></head>
<body>

<form action="ageist.php" method="post">

Input how old you are: <input name="age" size="2">
</form>
```

```
</body>

</html>
```

The message that is entered is shown by the "ageist" script depends on whether or not the age entered is more or less than 18.

```
<html>

<head></head>
<body>
<?php

// retrieve form data

$age = $_POST['age'];

// check entered value and branch
if ($yourage >= 18) {

    echo 'Please come in, happy hour is about to start!';

}

if ($yourage < 18) {

    echo "You're not old enough for the lounge, you can come back
when you're of age";
}

?>
</body>

</html>
```

Additionally, there is also the PHP if-else function, which is used to describe a chunk of code. Which will be performed when your expression that is conditional is false. Here is an example:

```php
if (condition) {

  Finish this!

  }

else {
finish this!

}
```

It can also be utilised in order combine two statements that are if into one statement that is referred to as if-else:

```php
<html>
<head></head>
<body>
<?php

// retrieve form data

$age = $_POST['age'];

// check entered value and branch

if ($age >= 18) {
    echo 'Come inside the lounge, it's happy hour!';

  }

else {
```

```
    echo "You're not old enough, sorry. Please come back when you
are of age";

}

?>
</body>

</html>
```

The next operator (which is the ternary operator) may confuse some people who are reading your PHP code. It is represented by a question mark. This symbol will allow you to create statements that are unperceivable, and it will provide you with shortcut syntax in order to create a statement that stands alone in the if-else chunk. One example of this is:

```
<?php
if ($numTries > 20) {
    $msg = Your account will be blocked...';

    }

else {

    $msg = 'Hello!';

}
?>
```
 Or , you can do something like this:

```
<?php
```

```
$msg = $numTries > 20 ? 'Your account will be blocked...' : 'HI!';
?>
```

You can also "nest" your statements that are conditional inside the statements.

If you're wondering how to tackle multiple possibilities, you can do that with the if-elseif-else construct. A typical example of this would be:

```
if (first condition is true) {

    do this!

}

elseif (second condition is true) {

    do this!

}

elseif (third condition is true) {

    do this!

}

    ... and so on ...

else {
```

```
    do this!

}
```

Chapter 4:
Delving Deeper

In this chapter we will go a little deeper into PHP's operators and control structures, such as two new operators, an alternative to the if-else ( ) family of conditional statements, as well as some of the loops. Let's begin with the alternative to the if-else control structures, which is PHP's switch-case ( ) statement. It does basically the same thing, and one example of this is:

```
switch (decision-variable) {
    case first condition is true:
        do this!
    case second condition is true:
        do this!
    ... and so on...
}
```

The appropriate case will be executed, depending on the value of the decision variable. You can also create a default block, and it can handle all of the times the value of the decision variable doesn't match any of the listed case ( ) conditions. Here is an example of one of the earlier statements utilising the switch ( ) statement:

```
<html>
<head></head>
<body>
<?php
// get form selection
$day = $_GET['day'];
// check value and select appropriate item
```

```
switch ($day) {
   case 1:
     $menu= 'Chicken Penne";
     break;
   case 2:
     $menu = "Minestrone soup';
     break;
<h2>Today's menu is:</h2>
<?php echo $menu ?>
</body>
</html>
```

There are some important things to remember here:

1) You use the broken keyword to break out of the statement switch and go towards the lines that come after it.

2) The default word will bring out a set of commands when your variable that is passed to the switch ( ) doesn't meet the needs of the conditions that are inside the block.

As a beginner, you may forget the pause at the end of the ( ) block. . Even if you forget to break out of the case ( ) block, the PHP script will keep executing the code in all of the case blocks ( ) that come after it.

When you are creating procedures in your PHP, you have to put the HTML code in a file, and then you will work with the form processing in your PHP script. On the other hand, conditional statements will allow you to combine both of them into one script. If this is your goal, you will have to assign one title to your submit code, and you can check if the menu $_POST variable has the title when you see the script. If the name is included and you submitted the form, then you can exhibit the data. If it hasn't been submitted, then you need to produce the first form. Therefore, you need to test if this variable is present or absent. One example of this is:

```
html>
<head></head>
<body>
<?php
/* if the "submit" variable does not exist, the form has not been
submitted - display initial page */
if (!isset($_POST['submit'])) {
?>
   <form action="<?php echo $_SERVER['PHP_SELF']; ?>"
method="post">
   Enter your status: <input name="status" size="2">
   <input type="submit" name="submit" value="Go">
   </form>
<?php
   }
else {
/* if the "submit" variable exists, the form has been submitted - look
for and process form data */
   // display result
   $maritalstatus = $_POST['statur'];
   if ($status >= single) {
      echo 'Fill out this application if you're single!';
      }
   else {
      echo 'It says you're married, I'm sorry but we are looking for
single people;
      }
}
?>
</body>
</html>
```

The script here has two pages, which are the initial, empty form and the page with the results that you get after pushing the submit button. Before the system decides which page to display, your script has to make sure that there is the $_POST ['submit] variable. If it is not there, the system will think that you didn't submit the form yet. It will submit the first list of information, and once you submit the form, the same script will process the input. Your submit button must have a value assigned to its "name" attribute, and you have to check for the value that is in the primary conditional statement. The $_SERVER array is a special PHP variable that will hold server information, and this includes the path and the name of the script that you are executing.

Now it is time to work with loops. A loop is a control mechanism that will allow you to repeat the same set of PHP statements or commands for as many times as you want. You can specify the amount of repetitions you want, and it can depend on the conditions as well. Before we go deeper into loops, you have to learn about the auto-increment operator which will automatically decipher the value of the variable it is attached to. You will recognize by two plus signs (++), such as :

```php
<?php
// define $total as 10
$total = 10;
// increment it
$total++;
// $total is now 11
echo $total;
?>
```

You will notice that the operators are used frequently in loops in order to update the loop counter's value. In addition, the easiest loop to learn is called the while ( ) loop, and it looks like this:

```
while (condition is true) {
    do this!
}
```

As long as the condition turns out to be true, the PHP statements with the curly braces will execute as planned. If it becomes false, the loop will break and the statements following the loop will be executed. There is an example of this below:

```
<html>
<head></head>
<body>
<form action="squares.php" method="POST">
Print all the squares between 1 and <input type="text" name="limit" size="4" maxlength="4">
<input type="submit" name="submit" value="Go">
</form>
</body>
</html>
```

There is an easier form which requires you to put in a number. Once you submit the form, the PHP script that you input the number into will print the squares of all the numbers between 1 and your entered number. An example of this is:

```
<html>
<head></head>
<body>
<?php
```

```php
// set variables from form input
$upperLimit = $_POST['limit'];
$lowerLimit = 1;
// keep printing squares until lower limit = upper limit
while ($lowerLimit <= $upperLimit) {
    echo ($lowerLimit * $lowerLimit).' ';
    $lowerLimit++;
}
// print end marker
echo 'END';
?>
</body>
</html>
```

The script will use a while ( ) loop which will move forwards from one until the values of $lowerLimit and $upperLimit become equal. The while loop will generate one set of statements, if a condition is true. However, if you were to enter the value 0 in in the form, the while loop won't execute. If you need to execute a bunch of statements once, PHP will give you the do-while loop. Here is an example of that:

```
do {
    do this!
} while (condition is true)
```

Here is another that demonstrates the example that will help you understand the difference between while ( ) and do-while ( )

```php
<?php
$x = 100;
// while loop
while ($x == 700) {
```

```
   echo "Running...";
   break;
}
?>
```

You should notice that it doesn't matter how many times you want to run the script, because you will get no output, because the value of $x is in unequal to 700. However, you can run the script like this:

```
<?php
$x = 100;
// do-while loop
do {
   echo "Running...";
   break;
} while ($x == 700);
?>
```

You may notice that there is one line of the output, because the code with the do ( ) block will run once now. Furthermore, both the while ( ) and do while ( ) loops will work as long as the conditional expression that you specified is true. However, if you need to execute a certain number of statements for a certain number of times, then you will have to use the for ( ) loop, which looks like this:

```
for (initial value of counter; condition; new value of counter) {
   do this!
}
```

It may look confusing, but the "counter" is a PHP variable that is designated to a numeric value, and it will keep track of the number of times that you execute the loop. Before you execute the loop, the "condition" will be tested. If it is true, the loop will execute once more, and the counter will be put in accurately. If is false, the loop will break and the lines after it will be executed. This is how you can use the loop:

```
<html>
<head>
<basefont face="Arial">
</head>
<body>
<?php
// define the number
$number = 13;
// use a for loop to calculate tables for that number
for ($x = 1; $x <= 10; $x++) {
   echo "$number x $x = ".($number * $x)."<br />";
}
?>
</body>
</html>
```

There is another way you can use loops that will prove its usefulness. It also exemplifies how practical and useful PHP programming can be.

```
<html>
<head></head>
<body>
<form method="post"
action="<?php echo $_SERVER['PHP_SELF']; ?>">
Enter number of rows <input name="rows" type="text" size="4">
and columns <input name="columns" type="text" size="4"> <input
type="submit" name="submit" value="Draw Table">
</form>
<?php
```

```php
if (isset($_POST['submit'])) {
    echo "<table width = 90% border = '1' cellspacing = '5' cellpadding
= '0'>";
    // set variables from form input
    $rows = $_POST['rows'];
    $columns = $_POST['columns'];
    // loop to create rows
    for ($r = 1; $r <= $rows; $r++) {
        echo "<tr>";
        // loop to create columns
        for ($c = 1; $c <= $columns;$c++) {
            echo "<td> </td>
";
        }
    echo "</tr>
";
    }
    echo "</table>
";
}
?>
</body>
</html>
```

If you have ever tried coding by hand, then you may be pleased to know that PHP's for ( ) loop will save you lots of time, and it will make your coding much easier. It is also formatted neatly, and there are breaks at the end of each table. Loops can be also used in combination with some complex data types, which are called an array. Arrays, loops, and forms all work together. So what exactly is an array? It is a complex variable that will let you store multiple values in a single variable. This will benefit you when you need to store and represent related information. One example is:

```php
<?php
// define an array
$pizzaToppings = array('onion', 'tomato', 'cheese', 'green
peppers', 'chicken', 'olives');
print_r($pizzaToppings);
?>
```

The "pizza toppings" is an array variable , and it contains the values "onion", "tomato" "cheese" "green peppers" "chicken" and "olives" . Arrays are good to use when you group related values together. Print_r ( ) is a special function that allows you to look inside an array. You can also use it for debugging (in order to see if your script is working) and it can be used for display purposes. You can access the various elements of the array with an index number. The first element starts at zero. For example, if you access the element "onion", then you would use the notation $pizzaToppings[3] , while "chicken" would be $pizzaToppings [3] . PHP will also let you replace indices with "keys" that are user-defined. It will create a different type of array. Each one is unique, and it corresponds to a single value in the array. One example is:

```php
<?php
// define an array
$fruits =
array('red' => 'apple', 'yellow' => 'pepper', 'purple' => 'eggplant, 'gre
en' =>'olives');
print_r($food);
?>
```

In this example, $fruits is an array variable that contains four key-value pairs. The => symbol will indicate the association between a key and its value. If you want to access the value "pepper", you would use the notation:

$food['yellow'], while the value 'olives' would be accessible via the
notation $food['green'].

This type of array can sometimes be called a "hash" or "associative array". The easiest way to define an array variable is the array ( ) function. One example is:

```php
<?php
// define an array
$pasta = array('spaghetti', 'penne', 'Gnocchi');
?>
```

You would follow the same rules for choosing an array variable name as any other PHP variable. It has to begin with a letter or underscore, and it can be followed by more letters, numbers, and underscores. Alternatively, you can define an array when you specify values for each element in the index notation, such as this example:

```php
<?php
// define an array
$pasta[0] = 'spaghetti';
$pasta[1] = 'penne';

$pasta[2] = 'Gnocchi';
?>
```

If you like to use keys instead of the default numeric indices, you might want to try something like this:

```php
<?php
// define an array
$menu['breakfast'] = "scrambled eggs";
```

```php
$menu['lunch'] = "chicken sandwich";
$menu['dinner'] = 'penne';
?>
```

You can add the elements to the array the same way. If you wanted to add something like "anchovies" to the pizzatoppings array, you can use something like this:

```php
<?php
// add an element to an array
$pizzaToppings[3] = 'anchovies";
?>
```

If you want to modify the element of an array, then all you have to do is assign a new variable to the matching scalar variable. For example, if you want to replace "chicken" with "beef", then you can use:

```php
<?php
// modify an array
$pizzaToppings[4] = 'chicken';
?>
```

You can do the same when using keys. In the following example, it adjusts the element with the key "lunch" to a different value, like in this example:

```php
<?php
// modify an array
$menu['lunch'] = beef;
?>
```

Moreover, you can add an element to the end of an array with the array_push ( ) function, such as:

```php
<?php
// define an array
$pasta = array('spaghetti', 'penne', 'Gnocchi');
// add an element to the end

array_push($pasta, 'tagliatelle');
print_r($pasta);
?>
```

You can also remove an element from the end of an array using the array_pop ( ) function like in this example:

```php
<?php
// define an array
$pasta = array('spaghetti', 'penne', 'Gnocchi');
// remove an element from the end

array_pop($pasta);
print_r($pasta);
?>
```

If you need to take off an element from the top of the array, you can use the array_shift ( ) function:

```php
<?php
// define an array
$pasta = array('spaghetti', 'penne', 'macaroni');
// take an element off the top

array_shift($pasta);
print_r($pasta);
?>
```

The array_unshift ( ) function will add elements to the beginning of the array:

```php
<?php
// define an array
$pasta = array('spaghetti', 'penne', 'Gnocchi);
// add an element to the beginning

array_unshift($pasta, 'tagliatelle');
print_r($pasta);
?>
```

The array_push ( ) and array_unshift ( ) functions will not work with associative arrays, so if you want to use the $arr[$key] = $value notation to add additional values to an array. Furthermore, the explode ( ) function will split a string into smaller sections. This is based on a user-specified delimiter, and it will return the elements to as part of the array. For example,

```php
<?php
// define CSV string
$str = 'red, blue, purple, orange';
// split into individual words

$colors = explode(', ', $str);
print_r($colors);
?>
```

If you want to reverse it, you can use the implode ( ) function, which will create a single string from all of the elements in your array. It will join them together with a user-defined delimiter. So the reverse will be:

```php
<?php
// define array
$colors = array ('red', 'blue', 'purple, 'orange');
```

```php
// join into single string with 'and'

// returns 'red and blue and green and yellow'

$str = implode(' and ', $colors);
print $str;
?>
```

The two examples exemplify how the sort ( ) and rsort ( ) functions will be used to organize an array in an alphabetical or a numerical order. You can also do it in an ascending or descending order. For example,

```php
<?php
// define an array
$pasta = array('spaghetti', 'penne', 'Gnocchi');
// returns the array sorted alphabetically

sort($pasta);

print_r($pasta);

print "<br />";
// returns the array sorted alphabetically in reverse
rsort($pasta);

print_r($pasta);
?>
```

Now we will learn how to get the data in an array out. All you have to do is access the right element of the array using its index number. If you want to read an entire array, you can simply loop over it. You can do this by using any of your loop constructs, for example:

```
<html>

<head></head>
<body>
My favourite bands are:

<ul>
<?php
// define array

$artists = array('TheBeatles', 'Coldplay', 'U2, 'TheRollingStones');
// loop over it and print array elements

for ($x = 0; $x < sizeof($artists); $x++) {

   echo '<li>'.$artists[$x];
}
?>
</ul>

</body>

</html>
```

This is what you should see when you run the script:

My favorite bands are:

- The Beatles
- Coldplay
- U2
- The Rolling Stones

You have defined an array, and you also used it for ( ) loop to run through the script, extract the elements using the index notation. You should also display them in a sequence. Furthermore, you should make note of the sizeof ( ) function.

It serves an important purpose, and it is used often in array functions. It returns the size of (read: number of elements within) the array. You will use it a lot in loop counters in order to make sure the loop repeats as many times as there are elements in the array.

If you're using an associative array, the array_keys ( ) and array_values( ) functions will be useful to you. If you want to get a list of all the keys and values within the array. For example:

```php
<?php
// define an array
$menu = array('breakfast' => "scrambled eggs", 'lunch' => chicken
sandwich', 'dinner' =>'chickenpenne');
/* returns the array ('breakfast', 'lunch', 'dinner') with numeric
indices */

$result = array_keys($menu);

print_r($result);

print "<br />";
/* returns the array ("scrambled eggs", "chicken sandwich, 'chicken
penne') with numeric indices */

$result = array_values($menu);

print_r($result);
?>
```

If you want to make it even easier to extract all the elements of an array, PHP 4.0 has a new loop form that is created to repeat over an array. The foreach ( ) loop. It looks like this:

```php
foreach ($array as $temp) {
```

```
    do this!

}
```

A foreach ( ) loop runs once per element in an array, that is moving forward through the array on each repetition. This is not the case in a for ( ) loop, which doesn't need a counter or a call to the sizeof ( ). It is able to keep track of its position in the array on its own. On each of your runs, the statements within the curly braces are executed. The array elements that are currently chosen are made available in a temporary loop variable. This is a rewrite of the earlier example, which uses the foreach( ) loop:

```
<html>

<head></head>
<body>

My favourite bands are:

<ul>
<?php
// define array

$artists = array('TheBeatles', 'Coldplay', 'U2', 'TheRollingStones');
// loop over it

// print array elements

foreach ($artists as $a) {

    echo '<li>'.$a;

}
?>
```

```
</ul>

</body>

</html>
```

You may notice that every time the loop executes, it will place the array that you currently selected in the temporary variable $a. This variable can now be used by the statements inside the loop block. Since a foreach() loop doesn't require a counter to keep tabs on where it is in an array, it makes it easy to work with, and it is easy to read. You can also use it with associative arrays, and it doesn't need additional programming. So what else can it do? As alluded to earlier, arrays and loops can help you when you're processing forms in PHP. For instance, if you have a group of related boxes or a multi-select list, you will be able to use an array to capture all of the selected form values in one variable. This will make processing easy for you, and you can see that in this example:

```
<html>

<head></head>
<body>
<?php

// check for submit
if (!isset($_POST['submit'])) {

    // and display form

    ?>
    <form action="<?php echo $_SERVER['PHP_SELF']; ?>"
method="POST">
```

```php
<input type="checkbox" name="artist[]" value="TheBeatles">The
Beatles

<input type="checkbox" name="artist[]"
value="Coldplay">Coldplay

<input type="checkbox" name="artist[]" value="U2">U2

<input type="checkbox" name="artist[]" value="The Rolling
Stones" The Rolling Stones
<input type="checkbox" name="artist[]" value="The
GOASTT">The GOASTT

<input type="checkbox" name="artist[]" value="M83">M83
<input type="submit" name="submit" value="Select">
</form>
<?php

}

else {

// or display the selected artists

// use a foreach loop to read and display array elements

if (is_array($_POST['artist'])) {

    echo 'You selected: <br />';
    foreach ($_POST['artist'] as $a) {

        echo "<i>$a</i><br />";

    }

}
```

```php
    else {

        echo 'Nothing selected';

    }

}

?>
</body>

</html>
```

When you submit something like the form listed above, PHP will automatically create the array variable, and add the items that you selected. This array can be processed with a foreach ( ) loop, as well as the selected items that are retrieved. You can even do this with a multi-select list, and you can do this by using an array notation in the select control's "name" attribute.

Chapter 5:
Working With Filing

In this chapter, you will learn how to open a file and how to read its contents. You can pretend that somewhere on your disk, you have a text file that contains the recipe for Japanese cucumber salad. You would like to read the information on this file and put it into a PHP script. There are a few easy steps to do this, and they are:

1. Open your file and give it a file handle - Every PHP needs a file handle to read the data from a file. You can create the fopen( ) function. It will accept two arguments, the name, and the path to a file as well as a string. The string will indicate the "mode" that you need to open the file with. There are three different modes that you can use with the fopen ( ) function. The list is:

   "r"- this will open a file in read mode

   "w"- this will open a file in write mode, and it will destroy the contents of the existing file

   'a" – This opens your file in append mode, which means it will preserve the contents of the existing file.

2. Go into the file using the handle, and you can extract the contents into a PHP variable. – if your fopen ( ) function is correct, it will return a file handle, $fh, which will be used to further interact with your file. The file handle is used by the fread( ) function, and it will read the file and place the contents into a variable. The second argument is the number of bytes that you need to read, and you can get this information through the

filesize( ) function. This will lower the size of your file in bytes.

3. Close your file – You don't have to do this part, because PHP will close the file automatically it once it reaches the end of your script. However, it is good to get used to closing it. You can do this by using the fclose ( ) function, which has two benefits. It can clean up any loose ends in your script, and it is beneficial with PHP. Furthermore, there is the die ( ) function, which is used as a mechanism to fix errors. If there is a fatal error, such as your file is invalid or your PHP cannot understand the file permissions, the die( ) function will delete the script processing and it may display a user-specified error message explaining why it deleted the information.

Alternatively, you can also read data from the file ( ) function, which will read the whole file into an array with one line of code. Each element of your array will have one line from your file. In order to display the information in this file, all you have to do is copy over the array in a foreach ( ) loop, and then you can print each of your elements. This is an example:

```php
<?php
// set file to read
$file = '/usr/local/stuff/that/should/be/elsewhere/recipes/o
melette.txt' or die('Could not read file!');

// read file into array

$data = file($file) or die('Could not read file!');

// loop through array and print each line
```

```
foreach ($data as $line) {

    echo $line;

}
?>
```

You will note that the file ( ) command will open your file, read it into an array and close the file. All of this can be done in one movement. Each of your elements in the array will correspond to a line from your file. It will be simple to print the contents of your file, and all you have to do is use the foreach ( ) loop. If you don't want the data in the array, you can attempt to get the file_get_contents ( ) function. This is new in PHP 4.3.0 and PHP 5.5 , which will read all of your file on one string.

This is an example:

```
<?php
// set file to read
$file = '/usr/local/stuff/that/should/be/elsewhere/recipes/Japa
neseCucumberSalad.txt' or die('Could not open file!');
// open file

$fh = fopen($file, 'r') or die('Could not open file!');

// read file contents

$data = fread($fh, filesize($file)) or die('Could not read file!');
// close file

fclose($fh);

// print file contents
```

```
echo $data;
?>
```

You can try running the script through your browser, and the PHP should bring back your contents in the file. An example of this is:

```html
<html>

<head>

<title><?php echo $page['title'];?></title>
</head>

<body>

<!-- top menu bar -->

<table width="90%" border="0" cellspacing="5"
cellpadding="5">

<tr>

<td><a href="#">Home</a></td>

<td><a href="#">Site Map</a></td>
<td><a href="#">Search</a></td>

<td><a href="#">Help</a></td>

</tr>

</table>

<!-- header ends -->
```

Once you have done that, you can make the footer with the copyright notice in a second file called footer.php

```
<!-- footer begins -->

<br />
<center>Your usage of this site is subject to its published <a
href="tac.html">terms and conditions</a>. Data is copyright
Big Company Inc, 1995-
<?php echo date("Y", mktime()); ?></center>
</body>

</html>
```

Now you can create a script to display the content of your site, and include ( ) the header and footer at the appropriate times. See the example below:

```
<?php
// create an array to set page-level variables
$page = array();

$page['title'] = 'Product Catalog';

/* once the file is imported, the variables set above will become
available to it */
// include the page header

include('header.php');
?>

<!-- HTML content here -->
<?php
// include the page footer

include('footer.php');
```

```
?>
```

When you run your script , PHP will automatically read the header and footer files. It will merge them with the HTML content, and it will show you the entire page. You can even write the PHP code inside of the files that are being imported. When the file is read, the parser will look for any php tags, and then it will execute the code inside of it. PHP will also offer the require_once ( ) and include_once ( ) functions which will make sure that a file that has already been read won't be duplicated. This will be useful if you want to delete multiple reads of the same file. This can be for performance reasons, or if you want to save space. In addition, the difference between the include ( ) and require ( ) functions is that the require function will bring back a fatal error. If the required file cannot be found, it will stop the script processing. The include ( ) function will give you a warning, but the script processing will continue.

The next step is a little more advanced, and it is writing to a file. The steps you use to write data are very similar to the steps involved in reading a file. You begin by opening the file and obtained a file handle. You use the file handle to write the data you need, and then you can close the file. However, there are two main differences. First of all, you have to open the fopen ( ) the file in the write mode. The second thing you have to do is the use the fread ( ) function to read from the file handle. You can use the fwrite ( ) function to write it, and you can see that in this example:

```php
<?php
// set file to write
$file = '/tmp/dump.txt';

// open file
```

```php
$fh = fopen($file, 'w') or die('Could not open file!');
// write to file

fwrite($fh, "I created a file!"
") or die('Could not write to file');

// close file

fclose($fh);
?>
```

Once you write this script, it should create a file under the name dump.txt in / tmp. Write a line next to it, and make sure there is a carriage return at the end of it. In addition, the double quotes will convert it into a carriage return. The fopen ( ), fwrite ( ) and fread ( ) functions are all safe binary codes. Therefore, you won't have to worry about damage to any of your files.

The following step will teach you the file_put_contents ( ) function, which takes a string and writes it in a file with a single line of code. For example,

```php
<?php
// set file to write
$filename = '/tmp/dump.txt';

// write to file
file_put_contents($filename, "I created a file!"
") or die('Could not write to file');
?>
```

The directory that you use to create the file must be created before you write to it. Moreover, PHP comes with functions

46

that will allow you to test the status of a file. You can find out if it still exists, if it is empty, or if it is readable or writable. You can even check if it is a binary or text file. The most common one is the file_exists ( ) function, and this tests if a specific file exists. Below is an example of when the user enters the path to a file in a Web form, and then it will return a message showing you if the if the file exists:

```php
<html>

<head>
</head>

<body>
<?php

// if form has not yet been submitted

// display input box

if (!isset($_POST['file'])) {

?>
   <form action="<?php echo $_SERVER['PHP_SELF']; ?>"
method="post">
   Enter file path <input type="text" name="file">

   </form>
<?php

}

// else process form input

else {

   // check if file exists
```

```
// display appropriate message

if (file_exists($_POST['file'])) {
   echo 'File exists!';

   }

else {

   echo 'File does not exist!';

   }

}

?>
</body>

</html>
```

There are many more functions, and here is a short list:

1) Is_dir ( ) – returns a Boolean that will tell you if the specified path is a directory
2) Is_file ( ) – returns a Boolean that will tell you whether the file you specified is a regular file
3) Is_link ( ) – returns a Boolean that will tell you whether the file you specified is a symbolic link
4) Is_executable ( ) – returns a Boolean that will tell you if the file you specified is executable
5) Is_readable ( ) – returns a Boolean that will tell you if the file you specified is readable
6) Is_writable ( ) – returns a Booelean telling you if your file is writable

filesize() – It will give you the size of your file

filemtime() – It will give you the last time you modified your file

filamtime() – It will give you the last time you accessed your file

fileowner() – It will give you the name of the owner

filegroup() – It will give you the group file

fileperms() – It will give you the permissions of the file

filetype() – It will give you the type of file

The script will ask you for a file name as input and it will use the functions above to return the information:

</html>

Your output will resemble this:

File name: /usr/local/apache/logs/error_log

File size: 60000 bytes

File owner: 0

File group: 0

File permissions: 30000

File type: file

File last accessed on: 2015-23-04

File last modified on: 2015-23-04

File is a regular file

File is readable

So what can you do with these skills? Say you had a recipe, and you wanted to convert them into HTML, so it will look good on your website. For example:

Japanese Cucumber Salad:

The ingredients:

1) Two cucumbers that are medium-sized, or you can get a large English cucumber

2) ¼ cup of rice vinegar

3) 1 teaspoon of sugar

4) ¼ teaspoon of salt

5) 2 tablespoons of toasted sesame seeds

Method:

1) Peel the cucumbers and make sure you leave green stripes that alternate.

2) Slice them in half vertically, and take out the seeds

3) Cut them into very thin pieces. You should use a processor or a knife

4) Put a double layer of paper towels and squeeze out any moisture that is left from the cucumbers

5) Mix in the vinegar, sugar and salt in a bowl. Make sure it is all dissolved, and add in the cucumbers and the sesame seeds. You are now ready to enjoy this low-calorie, delicious salad.

So to convert it to HTML:

```
<html>

<head></head>
<body>
<?php

// read recipe file into array

$data = file('/usr/local/stuff/that/should/be/elsewhere/omelette.txt') or die('Could not read file!');

/* first line contains title: read it into variable */

$title = $data[0];

// remove first line from array

array_shift($data);
?>
<h2><?php echo $title; ?></h2>
<?php

/* iterate over content and print it */

foreach ($data as $line) {
    echo nl2br($line);

}

?>
```

```
</body>

</html>
```

You have used file ( ) function to interpret the recipe in an array, and you can assign the initial line (title) towards a variable. The title is shown on each page, and you can print all your lines on your screen in a straight line. There is no need to worry about line breaks, and will leave you with a HTML version of your recipe.

PHP also has two functions that can be very useful to you to import the files, and make them a script that is PHP. There are two functions, and they are called include and function. Both of them are used to take out the exterior files lock, and the barrel and stock inside the script. This is beneficial if you have a linked application with a broken code across the files in different locations. In order to understand this more, both of the functions are a good example. You can pretend you're on your website and you have one basic bar on your page, as well as a copyright notice at the bottom. You don't have to cut and paste each footer and header, you can import them on each of your scripts, and they will show up at the bottom and the top. This will make a slight change to your website, and it will be easier to use. You no longer have to worry about manually editing all of your files, you only have to edit two of them. You will notice that the changes will be visible right away on your site.

Becoming Functional

Once your script becomes more complicated, you may notice difficulties with the procedures, and you may be wondering how to make it more efficient. There are ways to do this, and there are times when a code wont' be in a line that is linear. It may jump all over your script, and it is done through a function called function. You will learn how to build functions, and use the functions as much as you need. It will make it more concise, and it will make things simpler for you. A function is a number of statements that will do a job, anywhere in the program. As you may already know, every language in every program has its unique functions, and it will allow you to express your own. One example is if you had a profit for the last year, and you wanted to inflate by 30%. You can create a function called Shareholders ( ) and it will finish the job for you. Another benefit with functions is that functions that are defined by you will let you separate your code into sections that are easy to understand. They are also easy to debug. Secondly, your functions will give you a linked program, meaning you can write some code one time, and it will keep using it more than once in the program. Thirdly, the functions will make completing amendments or updates easier for you. This is because you only have to do it in one place. This is an example:

```php
<?php
// define a function

function TheusualResponse() {

    echo "Go Away, I'm upset with you!<br /><br />";
}
// arguing with your sibling

echo "Hey, do you have to throw away all my favorite toys? <br />";

TheusualResponse();
// in a meeting
echo "Do you understand the changes we are making to this project,
in addition to the new project I just assigned you. We have a new
```

client to work with so the workload is going to increase. You'll have to work some overtime, and you will have to start earlier than usual. I'm sure you can do it, and you will get paid for it.
";
theusualResponse();
// at a party

echo "Hello, I think I know you from University?
";

TheusualResponse();
?>

The output will look like this:

Hey, do you have to throw away all my favorite toys?

Go Away, I'm upset with you!

Do you understand the changes we are making to this project, in addition to the new project I just assigned you? We have a new client to work with so the workload is going to increase. You'll have to work some overtime, and you will have to start earlier than usual. I'm sure you can do it, and you will get paid for it

Go Away, I'm upset with you!

This is a good example of how the function feature will let you use the same bits of code. The first thing you have to do is make sure an original function is defined, along with the keyword for the function. Your keyword is shadowed by whatever name you gave to the function. For example the one you used above is theUsualResponse( ). All of your coding in the program is linked to the function, and then it is put in the braces. Remember, your coding can have statements that are conditional, loops, and even calling other functions and functions that are defined by you. However, once you have defined it, you have to bring it out too. You can do this by calling it by the name. One example is this:

function thefunction_name (you can have function arguments if you want) {

   statement 1...

   statement 2...

   .

   .

   .

   statement 3...

}

Furthermore, you will notice that functions will print out the same comment every time you call on them. However, you can bring back different comments too when you call them. The first thing you do to accomplish this is enter an argument. An "argument" functions by putting in one placeholder which symbolizes one variable inside a function. You get the values from this variable when you run it from your program. Because your input will be different every time you call it, and it will also at the output. Below is an example of a function that has one argument, and it brings it back after it is calculated.

```php
<? php
// you can define your function here

function getCalculationhere($circumference) {
```

```
    echo "Circumference of the rink with the radius $circumference is
".sprintf("%4.5", (3 * $circumference* ()))."<br />";
}
// you can bring up your function along with the argument

getradius (15);
// you can call the function with a different argument

getradjus(25);
?>
```

You may notice that when you take the getradius() function and it is called with the argument, the argument is paired up with a placeholder variable $circumference in the function. It is then acted out by your code with the definition. These are only some of the things you can do with PHP programming, but this is a good way to get started with it, so you can get more comfortable with it. You will love the efficiency of it, and your programming will be much smoother with it.

Conclusion

Thank you again for downloading this book!

I hope this book was able to help you to become more proficient with PHP programming.

The next step is to get some more practice with it, and you can use it to design your own website.

Finally, if you enjoyed this book, please take the time to share your thoughts and post a review on Amazon. It'd be greatly appreciated!

Thank you and good luck!